MATTHEW

ONE GREATER THAN SOLOMON

10 Publishing
a division of 10 of those.com

First published in Great Britain in 2018

British Library Cataloguing in Publication Data

A record for this book is available from the British Library

ISBN: 978-1-912373-47-5
Designed by Diane Warnes
Printed in the UK

10Publishing, a division of 10ofthose.com
Unit C, Tomlinson Road, Leyland, PR25 2DY, England
Email: info@10ofthose.com
Website: www.10ofthose.com

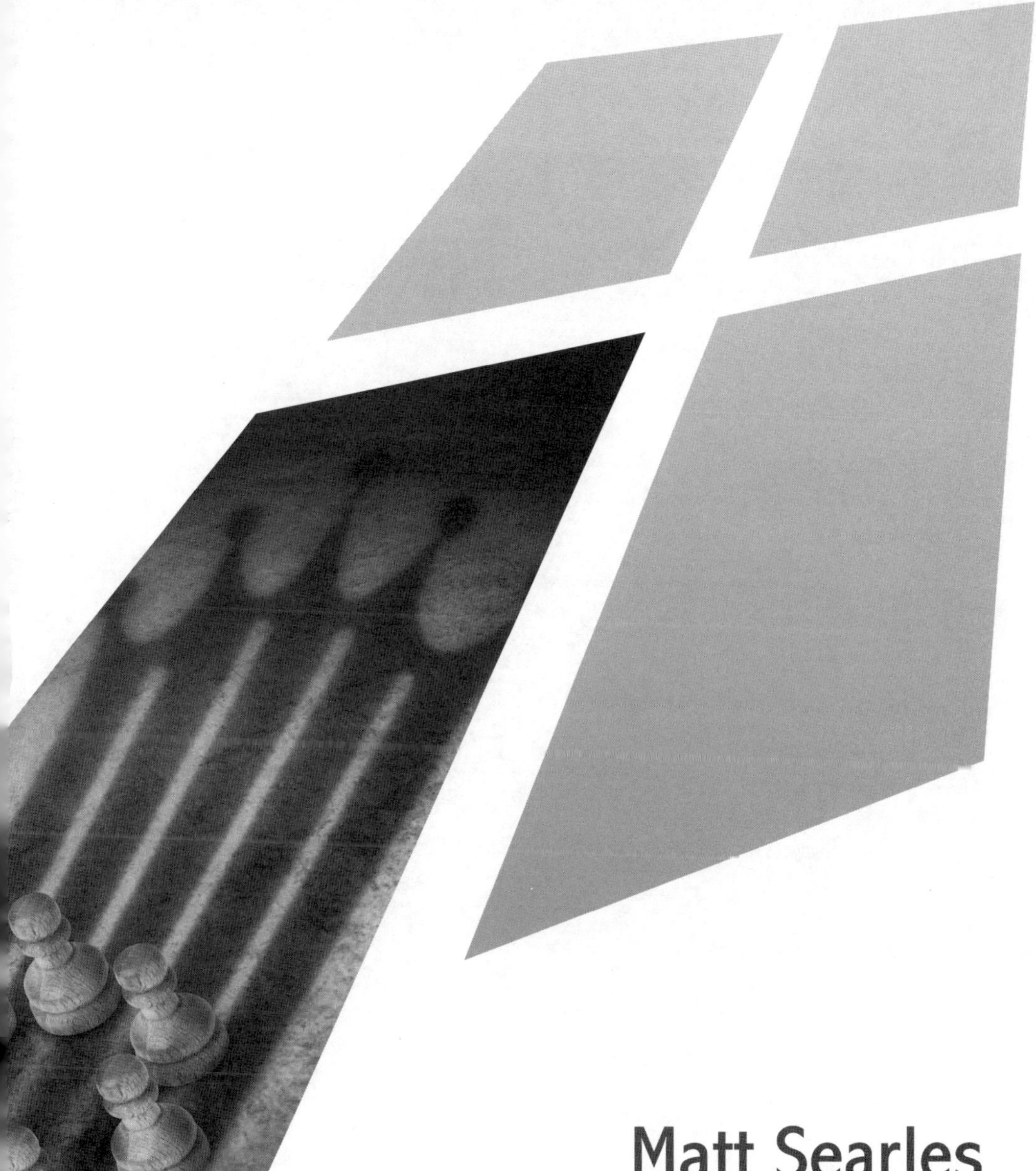

Matt Searles

46 UNDATED DEVOTIONS THROUGH THE BOOK OF MATTHEW

INTRODUCTION

What is the heart of the Christian faith? How would you summarise the good news? This is a question I often ask people, and it's a vital one to answer, whether we're looking into the Christian faith, or whether we've been Christians for years. How would you answer that question?

There are many wonderful things we might want to include. The hope of eternal life. God's great love for us. The fact that we're made acceptable to God by faith, not on the basis of any good we do. That we're all sinful and deserve judgment, but God has made a way for our sins to be forgiven. God as the good Creator. The gift of the Holy Spirit. The purpose God brings to our lives. An explanation of *grace*, and the *gospel*.

All of these are glorious truths, and ones I delight in daily. All are part of the good news of Christianity. But what is missing?

So far Jesus hasn't been mentioned. Though we'd never intentionally miss Jesus out, we must be careful never to divorce the great blessings that Jesus won for us from *Jesus himself*. He is the one in whom all these other things find their meaning. Yet I know my own heart can sometimes push him out of the picture a little, and focus on other things instead. This is one of the reasons I love the gospels. They take me back to Jesus himself. They put a Galilean carpenter front and centre.

Matthew's gospel is the most Jewish of the gospels, presenting Jesus as the fulfilment of Old Testament prophecies, the fruition of age-long hopes and yearnings. Though steeped in history, it is also profoundly contemporary as it presents a Jesus who is raw, confrontational, compassionate, majestic.

My prayer for this book of devotions is that it will help you to delight afresh in the one who is greater than Solomon. I pray that it will help you understand again why the promise 'They will see his face' (Rev. 22:4) is the highest and greatest joy the saints in glory can be offered.

We won't cover every passage in detail. Rather than being an exposition of all that is in the text, in each devotion I've tried to focus on one main theme, aware there's far more we could consider if we had extra time. My prayer is not so much that this helps you get to know Matthew's gospel better, but that it enables you to know *Jesus* better.

As you read the gospel, keep asking yourself the question: Who is Jesus? Keep on asking if the Jesus you believe in is as challenging, gracious, holy, gentle (and the list could go on) as the one presented by Matthew.[1] Keep praying that through this gospel God would give you eyes to 'see the king in his beauty' (Is. 33:17).

DAY 1

READ Matthew 1:1–17

'Things will be different when …' How would you complete that sentence? A new job, a new relationship, a new house? Debts paid off, a new pattern of eating or exercise? A new beginning can be a time of hope, of expectation.

Matthew's genealogy of Jesus is remarkable. It focuses on Jesus' legal ancestry (through Joseph instead of Mary) and points to new beginnings, new hope, blessing through a king in David's line. But who is this good news for?

Five women are included in the genealogy, which was not usual (foreshadowing how Jesus will treat women as equals despite his cultural situation). Rahab and Ruth were foreigners. All five women mentioned had some form of sexual scandal associated with them. Even the way Bathsheba is referred to as 'Uriah's wife' (v. 6) highlights the adultery and murder committed by David.

This is not a list of the spiritual greats, but a complete mix: heroes and villains, princesses and prostitutes, religious and non-religious. Not only are all these people non-western and non-white, but there is a positive emphasis on the foreigners: Tamar, Rahab, Ruth and Uriah.

These are the people in Jesus' ancestry. And these are the people Jesus welcomes into his family today.

If you've ever longed for a new beginning, if you are looking for things to change, if you know that life is not as it should be, this passage gives great hope. And it is a hope that is not restricted to the good, those with religious backgrounds, those with nothing to hide. This is a hope for people like you and me.

So come to him. Whether for the first time, or whether as someone who's been a Christian for years, come to him. Let him be the ultimate source of your hope. Let him be the new beginning you seek. Let him be your hope for a second, third, or three hundredth chance. His mercies are new every morning.

REFLECTION

What in our past or background makes us fear that Jesus won't welcome us?

How might God use flawed people like us to bring about his plans?

Jesus is not afraid to be numbered with prostitutes, murderers, foreigners and refugees. As a church, are we?

DAY 2

READ Matthew 1:18–25

Matthew's gospel is good news. Good news, as we saw in the first passage, for the sinful, the broken, the marginalised and the hopeless. It is a book heralding a new beginning, centring on the king who will come.

The two names given to Jesus in this passage are vital in showing what sort of a king he is. 'Jesus' was a common name meaning 'God saves', pointing to the hoped-for deliverance of the people from their enemies. Here a new feature is added: 'he will save his people *from their sins*' (v. 21, my italics). As will become abundantly clear in the rest of the gospel, Jesus is interested in more than just the spiritual; he wants to bring physical restoration to individuals and to the world. Yet all this must begin with the biggest problem being dealt with: human sin.

The second name is 'Immanuel', which means 'God with us' (v. 23). The people of Israel looked forward to a king who would come, but they didn't realise that this king would be God himself. God would no longer be distant, only *partially* known through the law, the temple and the sacrifices. God would walk among the people, making himself known to them. Think what a privilege it must have been to have walked the streets of Judea with Jesus. Imagine sitting listening to his teaching. In Jesus, 'God with us', we see not a distant god of the philosophers, but a God who came to earth so we could get to know him; he wants relationship with us. This privilege was not just for the disciples of Jesus' day; Matthew's gospel ends with this same promise: 'And surely I am with you always, to the very end of the age.'

REFLECTION

How aware are you of the presence of God with you at every moment of the day? How might you enjoy this reality more?

DAY 3

READ Matthew 2:1–23

Matthew's gospel begins with the promise of a new start. For many of us, however, a new start feels like simply the chance to make the same mistakes all over again.

This had been Israel's experience in the Old Testament. So much hope, so many fresh starts, yet still the same old failures.

Matthew does present a new start for Israel. But he does it by showing that *Jesus* will relive Israel's history, except he will do it right. He will be faithful where Israel was faithless. He will truly bring the people back from exile into the blessing of God. He will truly make all things new.

This section makes multiple references to Jesus fulfilling Old Testament prophecy. In particular, his flight into Egypt parallels the history of the people of Israel, who went down into Egypt. Likewise, Israel also experienced an atrocious infanticide when Pharaoh tried to wipe out the people of God through killing their babies. Jeremiah picked up on this image to describe the exile in similar terms, with the mothers of Israel ('Rachel') weeping over the loss of their children to Babylon (v. 18).

Jesus re-enacts the history of Israel. He goes down into Egypt but comes out, showing he is the redeemer who will release his people from bondage to slavery. He is the one who goes into exile but then returns, showing he is the one who will lead his people back into relationship with God and his blessing.

What comfort for the people! To know that their hope was not ultimately tied up to their faithfulness (or lack of it) but in the faithfulness of another. To know that there is a 'do-over' for their past mistakes – but it is Christ who will do this, who will make up for their shortcomings, who will live the life of faithful obedience God always wanted, and who will bring them with him into the paradise and blessing of God!

REFLECTION

Have you ever thought that Jesus deals with not just our past sins, but our future failures too?

How else do we see Jesus getting it right where Israel got it so wrong?

DAY 4

READ Matthew 3:1–17

God's judgment is a reality, no matter how much our society today tries to deny the fact. This was the heart of John the Baptist's message. The Pharisees and Sadducees are warned against presumption (v. 9) and this holds for us today. Like the people then, we are given fair warning that no religious affiliation will be any use on that day of the Lord's judgment. The kingdom of heaven has come near, which means the king has come near, and he will judge his enemies. The axe is already at the root of the trees.

John's message is one of rebuke to the presumptuous, yet it is also one of great hope to those who confess their sins. Matthew sees John's ministry as preparing the way for the Lord, quoting from Isaiah 40:3. Isaiah 40 continues by speaking of the comfort that will come to God's people after judgment has passed; the blessing of the restored reign of God. Judgment is a reality, but there is salvation beyond judgment, or rather, salvation *through* judgment.

Baptism is a sign of this. Just as Noah was saved through the waters of the flood, and the Israelites fleeing Egypt were saved through the waters of the Red Sea, so baptism pictures being saved through the waters of judgment.

The words spoken by the Father at Jesus' baptism capture these two aspects of his gospel message. 'This is my Son' (v. 17) identifies Jesus as the King of Psalm 2 who will judge the nations in his wrath. '... with him I am well pleased' identifies Jesus as the suffering servant of Isaiah 42:1–4, who would experience judgment on himself, so that the people might be saved. Judgment and salvation are bound together in the gospel; in fact they *are* the gospel. What God has joined together, let no one separate.

REFLECTION

Which aspect of Christ's character do you most need to dwell on?

How should future judgment impact how we live our lives today?

DAY 5

READ Matthew 4:1–25

The Christian life is hard. You don't need to have been a Christian very long to be aware of struggles with sin, temptations and failures. So many voices cry out to us – from the TV, our smartphone, our society – all luring us away from wholehearted obedience to Jesus. Yet this is nothing new. Read the Old Testament and you see God's people, Israel, constantly failing through hard-heartedness and unbelief. It is hard being a believer.

Again Matthew presents Jesus as succeeding where Israel failed. Israel was tempted for forty years in the wilderness, and rebelled. Here Jesus is tempted for forty days and nights in the wilderness, but remains faithful.

First, Satan tempts Jesus with **comfort**. After forty days without food, Jesus would have been on the point of starvation. The second temptation touches on identity and **recognition**: Satan offers Jesus the opportunity to have his glory revealed and seen by all, rather than be known as simply the carpenter. Thirdly, Satan offers **power** – all the kingdoms of the world and their glory. All these would have been very appealing, and Satan is even sly enough to tempt Jesus using the words of Scripture itself.

Where Israel spectacularly failed, Jesus spectacularly succeeds. We mustn't underestimate what it would have taken this fragile, hungry man to hold firm. We so often excuse our sin because our circumstances are particularly difficult. Jesus did not. Though his strength would have been all but spent after forty days without food, he knew that man does not live by bread alone, but on every word that comes from the mouth of God.

Of course there was something unique about Jesus' obedience, and we can rejoice that he – as the obedient Israel – is the one in whom all peoples will be blessed. We rejoice in his obedience *for* us. Our salvation is based on what *he* did, not on what we do. Yet still he says, 'follow me' (v. 19). Like him we can face temptations and trials by following his example of arming ourselves with Scripture, the sword of the Spirit by which we defeat the evil one.

REFLECTION

How could you intentionally memorise Scripture?

Try to find three verses to learn to help you in times of temptation.

DAY 6

READ Matthew 5:1–48

What is your attitude to 'law' in the Christian life? I write this on the eve of the 500th anniversary of the Reformation, when Luther rediscovered the glorious truth that our standing before God is not based on what we do, but on what Christ has done for us, received by faith alone. We are right to beware a legalism that thinks that our obedience to God's commands can earn us anything from God, or contribute in any way to our salvation.

But this doesn't mean that law and commands have no place in the Christian life. Just because the law can be misused doesn't mean it should be rejected altogether. Look at Jesus' attitude to law here in the Sermon on the Mount. Far from coming to abolish the law, he came to *fulfil* it. What this fulfilment looks like is explained in chapter 5: a *deepening* of the law to include more than just external behaviour, but heart attitudes as well.

'Do not murder' is broadened to include angry thoughts and bitterness. 'Do not commit adultery' is extended to include our thoughts, our desires and what we look at, and marriage is to be valued and treasured. 'Do not lie' becomes an all-encompassing requirement for truth in all we do. Jesus' teaching on 'going the extra mile' and loving our enemies is particularly provocative, especially in our culture where we stand on our own rights at all costs.

We could all think of a case (such as marital abuse) where an evil person *should* be resisted. The laws here aren't to be applied woodenly. Rather, they are more about what sort of person we should be. But this shouldn't dull the fact that as Christians we ought to be those who are known for 'turning the other cheek'. The 'hard cases' mustn't be used as a convenient excuse to escape the full force of this teaching.

If Christians lived more like this, wouldn't the watching world have so many more questions about the Christian faith? Wouldn't they want to ask about the hope Christians have that empowers such radical living? Of course the greatest example of this kind of living was Jesus Christ himself. In this sermon we see a picture of his glorious character. Who ever lived like this? Who is this man?

REFLECTION

Which command in this chapter is most challenging for you? Pray about that now.

DAY 7

READ Matthew 6:1–34

A true understanding of God as our Father is the antidote to both hypocrisy and worry.

We all know the ugliness of hypocrisy: someone who says one thing but does another; someone who is an actor (the original meaning of the word 'hypocrite') and pretends to be so much better than they are. It is an ugly sin, but it is one that tempts us all.

Here the hypocrites want praise from *people*. So they do their religious deeds – their giving to the needy, their praying, their fasting – very publicly so that they will be seen. If we're looking for praise from people, how tempting it will be to make out we're better than we are. We fear that if people really knew what we were like, maybe they'd reject us. So we pretend.

The solution is knowing God as *Father*. 'Father' indicates an existing relationship, so we don't need to try to earn our standing before him. 'Father' indicates love: we are loved and valued by God (v. 26), even though he knows our darkest secrets and our most painful weaknesses. 'Father' indicates his generosity (7:11). We don't need to earn anything from him, but still he delights in and even rewards our devotion to him.

Living to please other people is slavery, and leads to hypocrisy. Living to please our Father is perfect freedom.

Knowing God as Father also frees us from burdens of worry, and changes our perspective. We don't need to store up treasure on earth, and we don't need to worry about what we'll eat or drink or wear. Jesus isn't saying that these things aren't important – God knows that we need them, and here promises to provide them.

How sad when as Christians we bear unnecessary worry, because we forget we have a loving Father who cares for us, and provides for his children. How liberating when we live conscious of God as Father, and are freed up to seek first his kingdom and righteousness.

Get to know God as Father. Ponder his generosity. Live for his approval. Rest in his abundant grace.

REFLECTION

What do you need most in life? What do you crave? How does this passage speak to these things?

What aspects of God's fatherly care in this chapter do you most need to meditate on? Choose one verse from this section and make it your prayer today.

DAY 8

READ Matthew 7:1–29

When was the last time you threw away a Christian book? When was the last time you stopped listening to a sermon because it wasn't faithful to Scripture? It *matters* who we listen to, who we learn from.

The reason why is the stark nature of the alternatives Jesus paints at the end of the Sermon on the Mount. There are only two responses to him: two roads, two trees, two foundations. Our choice matters so much because of the destination set forth in verses 13 to 14: destruction or life.

Two roads (vv. 13–14). The road to destruction has a wide gate so people stumble onto it without thinking. More than that, it is an easy way, with no sacrifice. The gate to life is narrow in two senses: because Jesus is the only way to life, and because it will take a conscious decision to enter. We are all on one of these roads. To be agnostic is not to refuse to choose a way; it is just a different attitude to take on the road to destruction.

Two prophets, two trees (vv. 15–23). Not all who speak in Jesus' name should be listened to. This is the great danger of reading Christian books or listening to sermons online. They can be helpful – indeed a lifeline to some. But only in a local church can you truly see the long-term fruit of someone's teaching, both in their own life and in the lives of others. If the fruit is bad, then so is the tree. Are we discerning in choosing who we listen to? Even more terrifying is the possibility of self-deception. Some will say, 'Lord, Lord' (v. 22) and do great works in Jesus' name, but end up separated from God eternally.

The final picture of the **two builders** (vv. 24–29) further clarifies what it means to know Jesus. It is not hearing Jesus' words that counts; it is putting them into practice. If we are in patterns of hearing Jesus speak but then refusing to change our lives in response, we must question if we are not actually building on sand on the way to destruction.

REFLECTION

Are you on the road to life? How would you know?

Are you discerning in who you listen to? How can you be better at putting Jesus' words into practice?

DAY 9

READ Matthew 8:1–34

Jesus' miracles are often seen as being proof of his divinity: 'Only God could do that.' Is that how you view them?

At one level this is true, but it has problems. Such a view may assume that we all know what God is like already and Jesus' miracles are simply proving that he is divine. But Scripture teaches us that we all naturally have *wrong* views about God's identity that need correcting.

This is part of the reason Jesus came to earth: so that we might see God in the flesh; to make the invisible God made known to us. Matthew doesn't present Jesus' miracles so we can keep our existing notion of God and just decide whether Jesus matches up to it. Rather, Jesus is presented to us so we may know that *this is what God is like.*

In particular, chapters 8 and 9 of Matthew's gospel point us to the character of the kingdom Christ is bringing. We see that it is a fully-orbed picture of the restorative reign of God. Lepers are cleansed. The sick are healed. Storms are stilled. Those oppressed and broken by the powers of evil are restored. In the next chapter the blind will be made to see and the dead raised to life.

The coming of the kingdom of heaven is nothing short of the renewal of all things. It's not just the 'spiritual' aspects of life in view here, but the entire person. Nor is it just humanity that is restored; the created order itself will be put right. The calming of the storm is significant as in Jewish thinking storms and chaotic water were signs of oppressive evil and all that threatens God's people. All of this may be stilled with just a word from Jesus. This is the kingdom Jesus is bringing (experienced in part now, and fully when he returns.) This is what our God is like!

How will all this happen? How will this kingdom be established? Matthew places a quote from Isaiah at the centre of this section: 'He took up our infirmities and bore our diseases' (v. 17; Is. 53:4). This is from the famous 'suffering servant' passage. Jesus is the one who brings this restorative reign of God, but he will do it through being 'pierced for our transgressions … crushed for our iniquities' (Is. 53:5).

REFLECTION

Choose one story from chapter 8. How does it expand your view of God's character? How does it make you long for Christ's kingdom to come?

DAY 10

READ Matthew 9:1–34

How do we treat those who are clearly perceived as 'sinners'? Are our churches safe places for those whose lives are messy, shocking, depraved? Must people become socially respectable and conservative before they feel any hope of belonging?

How we treat 'sinners' reveals a great deal about how we view ourselves, and how we view the good news of Jesus.

In this section we see Jesus homing in on sin as the greatest problem that we all face. The story of the paralysed man coming to Jesus is shocking: surely we expect Jesus to *heal* the man. Yet Jesus focuses on the greater need: forgiveness of sins. Jesus isn't saying this man's paralysis is a result of his sin (and elsewhere Jesus discourages this line of thinking). Rather, Jesus is making a dramatic point that for *all* of us, sin is our greatest problem, even for those with other very pressing needs.

The universality of sinfulness, and Jesus' offer of welcome to all, is seen by who he calls. In the previous chapter he healed a Roman centurion's servant – remember that the Romans were occupying Israel at the time. He also healed a leper and two demon-possessed men, all of whom were considered unclean. Here in chapter 9 he eats with 'tax collectors and sinners' (v. 11). The religious establishment are appalled.

Jesus responds: 'It is not the healthy who need a doctor, but those who are ill' (v. 12). Jesus is the spiritual doctor, who came for those who are spiritually sick. If we think we are essentially good, we'll never see our need of Jesus. Maybe the Pharisees agreed with Jesus' statement in principle, but the way they acted towards 'sinners' showed that they actually thought themselves to be less spiritually needy. Often it is our actions that reveal our theology.

Jesus then quotes God's words through the prophet Hosea: 'I desire mercy [which could be translated 'love'], not sacrifice' (v. 13; Hos. 6:6). The sign of someone who has come to know Christ is not religious performance and external piety. Rather, it is love. Love for the one who forgave us even when we were appalling sinners. Love which is expressed in mercy and compassion to other 'sinners' like us.

REFLECTION

Dwell for a while on just how little we deserve from God, yet how extravagantly he has blessed us.

How in our home/family/ church can we seek 'mercy' and not 'sacrifice' this week?

DAY 11

READ Matthew 9:35 – 10:42

It's been said that we can organise our Christian lives around one of two questions: 'How does Jesus fit into my life?' or 'How does my life fit into what Jesus is doing?'[2]

Chapters 8–9 of Matthew have set out what Jesus is doing: bringing a kingdom which deals with evil, sickness, suffering and death. When Jesus looks at a world in need, he has compassion on it.

Faced with a world in desperate need, Jesus' strategy is remarkable: he sends his disciples. They are to preach the same message about this kingdom, they are to heal like he did, they'll even face the same opposition and unbelief as he did. There are aspects of this mission that are unique to the original twelve apostles. Nonetheless there are lessons that we can draw for our involvement in Jesus' mission.

The priority of prayer (9:38). One key indicator of what matters to us is what we pray about. If all we're concerned about is how Jesus can make our life better, we won't pray persistently for the gospel to reach a needy world. Conversely, praying for the world is one way to help us put God's plans at the centre of our lives. The book *Operation World* (or, as a more colourful version for children, *Window on the World*) would be a good way to do this.[3]

The reality of opposition (10:16–25). The disciples are to expect opposition: from religious leaders who want to preserve the status quo, from secular authorities who find the teaching of Jesus offensive, from family members who may disown them because of their faith in Jesus. The metaphor of being like sheep among wolves is a vivid one, and it applies to us today as we seek to make Jesus known.

Do not be afraid (10:26–42). Three times Jesus tells his disciples not to fear and points them to the future. God's people will be vindicated, so persevere with mission even when it is hard. God will one day judge the world, so press on in telling people of the only way of salvation. Jesus therefore declares, 'Whoever finds their life will lose it, and whoever loses their life for my sake will find it' (10:39).

REFLECTION

Which question organises your life?

How could you more intentionally pray for mission, both home and abroad?

Think of one situation where you could speak of Jesus. Pray for that now.

DAY 12

READ Matthew 11:1–19

Several years ago, with the backing of the British Humanist Association and prominent atheist Richard Dawkins, advertisements appeared on London buses reading, 'There's probably no God. Now stop worrying and enjoy your life.' The implication was that if God did exist, he would only be out to spoil our fun. What a contrast this is to the actual criticisms levelled at Jesus when he walked this earth.

John the Baptist had proclaimed the king who would come in judgment, bringing the great and terrible day of the Lord foretold in Malachi (Matt. 3:11; Mal. 4:5). Yet so far Jesus has come and shown compassion to the crowds, while he has left John languishing in prison. 'Are you the one who is to come, or should we expect someone else?' asks John (v. 3).

Jesus' response is striking: he doesn't point to just his power but also his *character*. Read verse five again: Jesus has great strength, but also cares for those who are weak. This looks back once more to Isaiah and the restoration God will bring. But John questions Jesus because of his patience, his delay before judgment, while the crowds criticise Jesus because of his indulgence (v. 19).

Do we hold together Jesus' utter frankness about the reality of judgment, yet also his patience and compassion for those who are lost? The message of grace is as scandalous, if not more, than the message of judgment. Jesus was criticised for partying too much, drinking too much, enjoying the good gifts of creation too much. He is nothing like the god that Richard Dawkins doesn't believe in.

Is this the Jesus we worship? Or have we sanitised him? Might any of the accusations levelled at Jesus be levelled at us? Is the message we believe really this good news? Look at Jesus afresh and be willing to change some of your preconceived ideas.

It's true that many are unprepared for the suffering that will be present in the Christian life. But many are unprepared for the great joys as well! 'Go ... report to John what you hear and see ... wisdom is proved right by her deeds' (vv. 4, 19).

REFLECTION

What aspect of Jesus' character here do you need to dwell on afresh?

What aspect of Jesus' character do your unbelieving friends need most to hear?

DAY 13

READ Matthew 11:20–30

Why don't people believe in Jesus? Some people say they would believe if God revealed himself to them through some miraculous sign. But he hasn't, they declare, so they remain unconvinced.

Sometimes Christians think that if we could find the 'silver bullet' argument – perhaps historical proof of the resurrection, or a great philosophical argument – we'd be able to convince people. Others think we just need to get our friends to hear the best speaker: maybe an insightful Christian thinker, or a sports or music star with real credibility. The passage today challenges these notions. Chorazin and Bethsaida are places where Jesus has done most of his mighty works. He has healed the sick, cast out demons, even raised the dead. He preached there, and with authority. Yet still they didn't believe. Think about that for a moment. Unbelief is *not* to do with lack of evidence, nor to do with the speaker. These things are not unimportant, but they're not decisive.

Why don't people believe? Verses 25–30 give two different answers. First, **God has hidden these things**. The identity of Jesus can only be seen by those whose eyes God has opened: 'no one knows the Father except the Son and those to whom the Son chooses to reveal him' (v. 27).

But second, there is another side to this. **The offer is made to all**: 'Come to me, all you who are weary and burdened, and I will give you rest' (v. 28). Those who don't believe in Jesus are those who refuse to come to him – those who see his wonderful deeds, and yet grumble about him. There is both divine sovereignty and human responsibility. We find it hard to hold them together. Yet Jesus doesn't see this as something to be embarrassed about. Rather, it is a cause for praise (v. 25.)

Our response? If you're not yet a Christian, come to him! Also recognise this is his world and that he is just to reveal himself to whomever he pleases. If you're a Christian, be humble! Next, pray that people may believe. Most of us probably do this already, knowing that God needs to open blind eyes. Then tell people the gospel – the offer is for all (v. 28). Finally, praise God. We live in a world where God is sovereign and all events, including who is ultimately saved, are in God's hands. That is a very good thing.

REFLECTION

How would you describe what we have seen so far in Matthew of the character of God revealed in Christ. Wouldn't you want someone like this in control?

DAY 14

READ Matthew 11:28 – 12:21

How does Jesus deal with the broken, the burdened, the weary? How does Jesus deal with those who feel they're barely hanging on, at the end of their resources?

Maybe we feel as if we're in this category? We have the pressures of work, or the lack of it. Pressure of caring for family, or of longing for such a situation. Pressure of trying to match up to our own expectations, let alone the expectations that others lay on us. And then if we're Christians, things are so much worse as we add a whole extra level of pressure, guilt and expectation from the church, and thus ultimately from God himself. At least that's how it often feels.

Here we see Jesus engaging with those who are struggling. His disciples are hungry, so he lets them eat. The religious establishment are furious, but Jesus again responds with the quote from Hosea: 'I desire mercy not sacrifice' (12:7).

Then he's in the synagogue and heals a man with a withered hand. 'But the law!' cry the religious leaders in effect. However, ahead of convention, Jesus cares about *people*. Jesus has come to do *good* (v. 12).

Has ever a man with such compassion walked the earth? Have we ever seen anyone so gentle? A bruised reed he will not break. How we need to hear that. To a burdened world, Jesus didn't come to lay extra burdens, but to give *rest*. Rest from the voice that says, 'You're not good enough.' Rest from the expectations of others that cripple us. Rest from the great enemies of sin, sickness and death.

Will we come to him? There are so many other places we might look for rest. Self-indulgence, or self-denial. Escapism that makes us forget for a while – whether through drink, drugs or pornography, or just the distraction of constant busyness, TV or socialising. Some of these are clearly illegitimate, some have their place. But none of them offer the true rest that Christ offers.

Maybe we need to see Jesus afresh. Do not view him as a cruel taskmaster – perhaps shaped by our experience of church and other Christians. But learn of him from Matthew's gospel: 'A bruised reed he will not break, and a smouldering wick he will not snuff out' (12:20).

REFLECTION

Ask yourself: Is this someone to whom I could bring my doubts, cares, sins, failures and griefs?

And: Is the Jesus I believe in and speak of as compassionate and gracious as the one presented in Matthew's gospel?

DAY 15

READ Matthew 12:22–50

There is nothing more central to the Christian life than getting the identity of Jesus correct. In this passage, as opposition to Jesus continues to mount, the question of his identity comes to the foreground.

It's remarkable that those who opposed Jesus didn't question whether he performed miracles or not. Rather, they questioned where he got the power to do so; they attributed his power to Satan – Beelzebul.

The principle that runs throughout this section is that a tree is known by its fruit (v. 33). This goes for Jesus himself: if he is casting out demons, he can't be working for Satan. If he is performing miracles that Isaiah associated with the pouring out of the Spirit, it is a sign the kingdom of God has come. Far from working *for* Satan, he is plundering his possessions, rescuing people from his dominion – just as the Israelites were rescued from slavery to Pharaoh so many years previously.

Jesus' actions reveal his identity. Think back to what you have seen of Jesus so far in Matthew. What picture is building up?

The actions of Jesus' opponents reveal something about them as well. Their rejection of Jesus reveals their evil hearts. They are committing the unforgivable sin, which is to see the works of Jesus first-hand, yet to attribute these to Satan not to the Spirit – blasphemy against the Spirit (v. 32).

We will all have to give an account for the words we've spoken. Jesus can even say, 'by your words you will be acquitted' – or condemned – on judgment day. This is because our words reveal our hearts.

Though the passage began with the spotlight on Jesus, it ends with the spotlight on us. One greater than Jonah is here. Have we turned to him in repentance? One greater than Solomon is here. Will we listen to him?

REFLECTION

Think back through Matthew's gospel so far. What have you seen to change or enrich your view of Jesus?

DAY 16

READ Matthew 13:1–52

Are you ever discouraged by the progress of the gospel in the West? Far from growing, many churches are shrinking. Many denominations seem to have abandoned biblical teaching. In our personal evangelism we so often meet apathy or hostility. Jesus' kingdom seems inconsequential compared to the world around us, and the message about Jesus seems so *weak*.

Matthew 13 is a series of parables about the kingdom of heaven, and these are words we need to hear today if we are not to be discouraged.

The parable of the sower explains the different responses to the message about Jesus. It explains why in Jesus' day there was such opposition to him, and it reminds us that there will be different responses even today as we seek to make Jesus known. Only one soil of the four will produce a crop – yet what a harvest! Persevere in telling the gospel because the result will be far more than we would dare to expect.

The parables of the weeds and the net speak of the mixed nature of the visible church on earth. There will be those who associate with God's people who are not themselves believers: they are weeds, or bad fish. For a time they may look like believers – and how hard it is when we face opposition from such people *within* the church. The bad will be separated from the good, but not until judgment day; this calls for patient endurance on behalf of God's people.

The parables of the mustard seed and the yeast alert us to the hidden nature of kingdom growth. We should not 'despise the day of small things' (Zech. 4:10). Though the kingdom of heaven may seem small at present, it will one day encompass the whole earth. In fact the last 2000 years have been an incredible story of worldwide growth of this kingdom – and the greatest is yet to come.

The parables of the hidden treasure and the pearl of great price make this all personal. This is a kingdom worth searching for, worth giving up anything for.

REFLECTION

Have you come to Christ and become part of his kingdom? If not, what is stopping you?

If you are a Christian, how could this passage encourage you in your mission and evangelism?

DAY 17

READ Matthew 13:53 – 14:36

Imagine being in the boat when Jesus walked on the water. Imagine then seeing Peter join Jesus on the waves. These events, and the feeding of the 5000, would have been events that imprinted themselves on the memory. But they were far more than just conjuring tricks, or demonstrations of power. They reverberate with Old Testament allusions, and point to Jesus' identity.

The feeding of the 5000 is the only miracle to be recorded in all four gospels. It should remind us of Moses providing food for the people in the wilderness: the manna and quail (Ex. 16). Jesus is showing himself to be the new and greater leader of God's people, who will lead them – not into the promised land of Canaan, but the glorious new creation.

When Jesus walks on the water, he does so 'Shortly before dawn' (v. 25), which means the disciples would have been battling the storm for over nine hours by this time. As in the calming of the storm passage, the sea was a symbol for Israel of danger and evil. But there are other Old Testament allusions.

Psalm 74 describes the Exodus events as crushing the heads of the sea monsters. The image of head-crushing comes from Genesis 3:15 when God told the serpent that there would be enmity between his offspring and that of the woman: 'he will crush your head, and you will strike his heel.'

So when Jesus walks on the water, he is acting out the trampling of evil that he would achieve. He is the long-awaited serpent crusher. He is the one to bring about the true and greater exodus, leading the people through the sea to the land of promise.

This makes Peter walking on the water even more amazing: was he too able to crush evil under his feet? Yes (Rom. 16:20)! But he must keep his eyes on Jesus.

Jesus is the new Moses who provides for his people, and leads them to the messianic banquet. Come and be satisfied in him (14:20). Jesus is the serpent crusher, who will make an end of all that threatens his people. Trust him (14:31).

And can we too walk on water? Absolutely. Every time we share the gospel with an unbelieving friend, every time we stand firm in the faith, the powers of darkness recede before us. In Christ we have the victory.

REFLECTION

Is our view of Jesus as big as the one presented here?

How does this passage help us as we face adversity?

DAY 18

READ Matthew 15:1–20

Try to complete the following sentence from 1 Tim. 5:8: 'Anyone who does not ... has denied the faith and is worse than an unbeliever.' Now look up the answer if you didn't know it.

If Paul's words surprise us, then so might Jesus' teaching in this passage. He is speaking about the different sins that might defile us. He says that it is not external things that defile, but what comes from within: our thoughts and our behaviour. For those prone to self-righteousness, the list in verse 19 is devastating. Who can be free of all these things?

What might surprise us is the sin that he focuses on: honouring our father and mother. It might not be high on our list of most important duties. It's certainly not something that is seen as important in our society, and our churches may not be so different.

The Pharisees had a tradition of devoting money and possessions to God. What could be more spiritual? What could be more pleasing to God? Yet because of this tradition, they were not providing for the material needs of their parents – they weren't honouring father and mother. Devotion to God in one area of life never excuses disobedience in another. This is true in all areas of life, but is applied in particular to the fifth commandment.

'I'm too busy serving God to honour my parents': we might not say it as starkly as this, but we might be living this way. Of course honouring our father and mother will look different at different stages of our lives. For those who have had absent or abusive parents, this command requires particular wisdom. But it is a command we must always obey. Students, are you so busy at church, in the Christian Union and at summer camp that you don't spend any time with your parents, or give them help at home? Young people considering Christian work, will you take seriously your parent's desire for you to gain secular experience first? Those with ageing parents, will you consider them as you choose where to live?

Let's be careful that our traditions, our church expectations, our ministry don't lead us to nullify the word of God.

REFLECTION

What does honouring your parents look like at your stage of life?

What 'religious' practices of yours might actually hinder this command?

DAY 19

READ Matthew 15:21–39

'Did Jesus just call that woman a dog?!' This was the question a non-Christian asked in the Bible study a friend of mine was leading.

Like the Christians in the group that day, have we become so familiar with the story that this doesn't shock us? Have we become so familiar with Jesus that he never unsettles or challenges us?

Jesus' words here *are* shocking. How do they fit with the extraordinary compassion Jesus has demonstrated elsewhere in the gospel?

At this point, Jesus has just arrived in the region of Tyre and Sidon. He is now outside Israel, among Gentiles: non-Jews. This explains Jesus' response to the woman: he says he was sent to Israel – the 'children' – not the unclean Gentiles, who he refers to as 'dogs'.

Yet this woman doesn't react as we might expect. She accepts the label of 'dog' – of being unworthy and unclean – yet still pleads for crumbs. Her hope is not in her worthiness, but in Jesus' generosity to let even dogs eat fallen crumbs.

And this is what happens. Jesus commends her faith, and heals her daughter.

But why go about things this way? Why so much confrontation? Jesus was giving the woman the chance to exercise her faith.

The rest of the passage shows Jesus performing the same compassionate healings and miracles in this non-Jewish area as he did in Israel. He is demonstrating that his kingdom is open to *all*, regardless of ethnic or social background. In fact this Gentile woman becomes a model to everyone of what genuine faith looks like. It begins with accepting a negative verdict on ourselves: that on our own we don't deserve anything from God. But faith also involves trust in a God who gives good things even to those who don't deserve them.

The woman is an example to us. If we refuse to let Jesus say anything negative to us, we will never experience his blessings. Jesus *confronts* before he comforts. But, like in the case of this woman, he confronts *so that* he can comfort. A Jesus who never offends us might seem appealing, but such a Jesus could not save.

REFLECTION

How does this story humble us?

How does it give us great hope?

DAY 20

READ Matthew 16:1–20

'Who do you say I am?' Jesus' question to Peter is one he asks all of us. If you're looking into the Christian faith, this is *the* most important question to consider.

Peter's confession of Jesus as the 'Christ' or 'Messiah' is the turning point in Matthew's gospel, the climax of the first half. Yet for many of us this may feel like reading a murder-mystery novel for the second time. All the suspense has gone, and we lose the impact of the 'big reveal'. Many of us already know that Jesus is the Messiah: he is the long-awaited king from the line of David. But if we're honest, this truth may leave us cold. It is little more than a statement to give mental assent to; it doesn't grip our hearts, or stir our emotions.

If this is your situation, make it your prayer as you continue to read through Matthew's gospel that God would reveal to you *what sort* of king Jesus is. We might need to learn again why a Messiah is such good news, and we'll see that in how Jesus acts. If we're not excited by Jesus being the Messiah, it means that our understanding of him is still deficient. That's not intended as a rebuke, rather as an encouragement to pray that God would use Matthew's gospel to help you see afresh 'the king in his beauty' (Is. 33:17). Another possible question to ask ourselves is this: if someone were to look at my life, what would they say about the identity of Jesus? My lips may say, 'He is the Messiah', but what does my life say?

Is he someone who is just a good teacher? Is he someone we simply rely on to give us life coaching? Or is he someone on whom we rest all our hopes and dreams?

Is he king of all? Are there areas of our lives where we don't let him reign? Do we act as if his kingship is limited to 'spiritual' matters, but not things such as money, anxiety, sex or parenting?

Is he a good king? Wouldn't it be wonderful for people to see us delighting to submit to his rule, and enjoying his goodness. Let's not relate to him as a cold and distant rule-maker, but as the kind and compassionate figure revealed in the gospel so far, the hope of the ends of the earth.

REFLECTION

Who is Jesus to you? How do you view him?

What role does he play in your life?

DAY 21

READ Matthew 16:21–28

The nature of the god we worship will determine what that worship looks like. The Canaanite gods Baal and Ashtaroth were fertility gods, and so their worship involved sleeping with temple prostitutes. The Norse gods were mighty warriors, and so their followers were called to pick up their swords in battle. The same is true of the gods that are worshipped today, whether the gods of other religions, or the gods of materialism or pleasure.

At this turning point of the gospel, Jesus reveals to the disciples what sort of Messiah he is. Then he immediately tells them how this will shape their discipleship.

'From that time on ...' (v. 21): from here on, the shadow of the cross looms large over everything Jesus says and does. He's been acknowledged as the Messiah, but he must show what sort of Messiah. Peter, along with most people of the day, expected a military leader who would defeat Israel's enemies, like David had done so many years ago.

Jesus will be this king like David, but he will also be the suffering servant of Isaiah 53, who will die for the sins of his people. Though we may well marvel and wonder that this is the way that Christ will achieve his victory, we should not be completely surprised. God has always been self-giving within the relationships of the Trinity. God has always been abounding in love, overflowing in his generosity. We will spend eternity pondering the depths of mercy shown at the cross, not because the cross reveals something new about God, but because it so clearly reveals the heart of who he is. If we don't understand the cross, we can know little of God.

Because of what Jesus is like, following him means taking up our cross and laying down our life in his service. We do this because we want to be like our Lord. He has *always* been self-giving, even from before the foundations of the world. At the heart of his Trinitarian being, God is a God of love, of other-person centeredness. Those who follow him are called to be like him – even to death, and to the glorious hope of resurrection beyond.

REFLECTION

Are there things you are holding on to in your life that you need to surrender to Jesus?

What practically can help you do this?

DAY 22

READ Matthew 17:1–8

What a thing to see God in his glory! Isaiah saw God in the temple and was overcome. Ezekiel had visions of God and was overwhelmed for seven days. Elijah had the Lord meet him on the mountain with earthquake, wind and fire. The first experience like this concerned Moses, who asked to see the Lord's glory at Mount Sinai. What a privilege as he ascended the mountain, was hidden in a cleft in the rock and the Lord passed by proclaiming his name. Yet even Moses could not see God fully or directly, for God said to him, 'you cannot see my face, for no one may see me and live' (Ex. 33:20).

This is some of the context we need to bear in mind as we consider the transfiguration. The splendour of the scene is hard to overestimate. Jesus is up a mountain, his face shining like the sun. Such an intensity of radiance and glory would have made it hard to even look at him. What was not possible in the Old Testament – even for Moses and Elijah – was now possible: a face-to-face encounter with God.

On earth Jesus was still fully divine, but his divinity was often hidden. Here we see him as he really is. What a privilege for Moses and Elijah, as well as the disciples, to see him in his glory, to know the direct and glorious presence of God.

God's words to Jesus are also hugely significant. He is the beloved Son (v. 5): the King of Psalm 2. He is the one with whom God is 'well pleased': the suffering servant of Isaiah 42. He is the great prophet of old (Deut. 18): so the people are urged, 'Listen to him!'

What is our response? The disciples fell on their faces, surely the only right response to the glory of God displayed in Christ. This God who revealed himself on that mountain in staggering majesty is the God who reveals himself with equal majesty in the pages of Scripture. Will we gaze on him in trembling and awe? Will we fall down on our faces in worship? Will we listen to his word, more certain than the words of the prophets? This is our God. Gaze on him. See the King in all his beauty.

REFLECTION

Spend some time reflecting on the majesty of this scene. Pray that God would use this passage to increase your view of Jesus.

DAY 23

READ Matthew 17:9–27

The scene the disciples have just witnessed could not be more glorious. It has been the 'mountain-top experience' to end all mountain-top experiences. They have seen God himself, Immanuel.

Perhaps their eyes were still dazzled by the brightness and glory of what they'd just witnessed. And their hearts would have been in ecstasy, knowing that the hopes of generations were being fulfilled. Standing before them was the one who laid the foundations of the earth, called the stars out by name and tamed the raging oceans.

Was this the great day of the Lord promised by Malachi? Was the Lord now coming to his temple (Mal. 3:1)? Was the day finally here when no root or branch of wickedness would escape the fire of judgment, when the wicked would be set on fire like stubble, and when the sun of righteousness would rise with healing it its wings? Malachi had promised that Elijah would return before that day, so the disciples are confused: have they missed him?

Jesus shifts the expectations of the disciples. All that they long for is beginning to be fulfilled, but not yet in the public and powerful ways they expect. John – the Elijah who was promised – was put to death and Jesus would follow him in this. This is how the great day of the Lord would be brought about. This is how Jesus will exercise his kingship. The transfiguration was a temporary revealing of Jesus' glory, but before its full and final revealing he would have to go the way of the cross and shame.

We see this further in the accounts that follow. Jesus is the glorious King to whom all worlds will bow, yet he shows his care for individuals like the boy with seizures. This is not a turning from glory. Rather, Jesus' glory shines all the brighter as he enters into the brokenness and suffering of the world.

Jesus is the one who called planets into existence, yet he is also personally and purposefully sovereign over the small details of life – even ensuring that someone would drop a coin and a particular fish would swallow it, then be in the right place to be caught, all to meet his people's need.

REFLECTION

Is our Jesus as glorious as the one portrayed here? Is he this big?

Is our Jesus as involved in the small details of life? Is he this close? Praise him!

DAY 24

READ Matthew 18:1–35

How do we treat the 'little people'? How do we treat those who are below us in status? Those younger than us or less intelligent than us? Those with fewer social skills, or greater physical or emotional needs than we have? Those with obvious sins in their past? Or those who don't fit in culturally, perhaps because they are of a different class or ethnicity? Do we make the gospel understandable to all, or is there a perceived minimum level of intelligence and education needed to be considered a true Christian and part of the fellowship?

The theme that runs throughout Matthew 18 is 'little ones'. It begins with the disciples asking about who is the greatest in the kingdom of heaven – no doubt assuming that they were near the top of the list. Jesus uses this opportunity not just to redefine greatness, but to explain faith itself. He doesn't use children as examples because of any supposed sinlessness, but because of their 'lowly position' (v. 4). To think that you are great or important or special is a failure to have the same humble trust as one of these 'little ones'.

Do we prize our status in the church? Do we think of ourselves as 'important' or 'strategic' for the kingdom? Remember the faith of these 'little ones'. Do we think the good news of Jesus is only for the intelligent, for those with a certain education, for those old enough to be able to answer our complicated questions? Remember the faith of the 'littles ones'.

Most of this passage is about how we treat others. We are to be ruthless about our sin, particularly sin that might lead others astray. Like God, we should care about every 'little one' at church who is wandering – just as the shepherd is not content that 99% of his flock is being looked after.

Where does the power to live like this come from? To see others rightly we need to see ourselves rightly. To treat others rightly we need to remember how God has treated us.

Let us make sure that we're not like the unforgiving servant, treating others badly because we forget just how incredible is the forgiveness we've received. As we meditate on the Lord's forgiveness and adore him for it, will we seek to be like him, and care for 'little ones', just as he cared for little ones like us?

REFLECTION

In what ways do we think we are 'great' in the kingdom of heaven? Who are the 'little ones' we most need to look out for?

DAY 25

READ Matthew 19:1–30

If you're reading this, there's a high chance you live in a developed country. A place of wealth and opportunity, provision and comfort. If this is the case, we should be unsettled by Jesus' teaching in this passage: 'many who are first will be last, and many who are last will be first' (v. 30).

Again children feature in this chapter: 'Let the little children come to me, and do not hinder them, for the kingdom of heaven belongs to such as these' (v. 14). This doesn't mean that all children are believers, but it does highlight the appropriate attitude of someone who wishes to be part of God's kingdom: *dependence*. Young children cannot make it in the world alone; they rely on their parents to provide what they need. So it is with Christian discipleship.

What a contrast to the man who then comes to Jesus asking about eternal life. He is different to the children in two significant ways. First, he is coming asking what he can *do* to gain eternal life. Jesus' answer is designed to show the man his inability to earn anything from God. No matter how many commands we are able to keep, there are always others where we fail. Salvation is never earned by good works.

But the real focus is on the second problem: the man's money. Jesus calls this man to sell all he has and give it to the poor (v. 21). For this man, money has taken the place that only God should occupy.

This radical command to give everything away is not repeated anywhere else in the Bible, so it is not a blanket command for all Christians. But if we're feeling particularly relieved by this, it might mean that, like the rich man, our wealth is getting between us and God, and so maybe Jesus *would* give the same command to us. Today so many of us have enough money to provide for our future, gain comfort in the present and to cope with the uncertainties of life. We have enough money that we barely need to depend on God.

How hard it is for a rich person to enter the kingdom of heaven. How hard it is for a rich person to have childlike, dependent faith!

REFLECTION

What is the biggest rival to God in your affections?

What would it practically look like to be radically generous in your giving? What might be the results? Plan a time now to prayerfully review your giving.

DAY 26

READ Matthew 20:1–16

It's been said we live in an 'entitlement' culture. We believe very strongly in our rights and we're quick to spot if we're not being given what we deserve or expect. We feel that society, the government, God, the world even, *owes* us.

How did you respond to the parable Jesus tells about the labourers in the vineyard? Read it again and have a think. Those who work the full day receive one denarius. Those who are hired at 5 p.m. receive a denarius also. What do we make of this?

This parable illustrates the kingdom of heaven, with God as the vineyard owner. How we respond to the parable will depend on which group of people we identify with. Do we see ourselves as those who have 'borne the burden of the work and the heat of the day' (v. 12)? Do we feel that because we've done so much for God, he should probably reward us a little more? Or do we feel like those hired at the end of the day, who've done pretty much nothing yet received so much?

Do we begrudge God's generosity to others? To other Christians, or even other churches that we think of as less faithful? Do we resent God's blessing them? If we're looking like this at others, it's because we've a wrong view of ourselves. We think we're the first group of workers. We think we've *earned* what we have from God. In fact we are *all* eleventh-hour workers, those who receive so much more than we deserve.

We've also a wrong view of God. The true antidote to entitlement is to understand the character of God: like the vineyard owner he is generous and loves to give good things. He never gives *less* than anyone deserves, but he delights to give *more*!

As long as we act as if we're the first group of workers, who *earned* what they got, we'll begrudge God's generosity, and be upset when others are blessed. Once we not just understand but live as if we're eleventh-hour workers, we'll rejoice in our undeserved blessings and God's extraordinary generosity.

REFLECTION

When are we tempted to whisper to God, 'You owe me'?

Do we begrudge God's generosity to other believers? Who? Why?

DAY 27

READ Matthew 20:17–34

Here we have one of the most important – and challenging – passages on Christian leadership and ministry. While particularly relevant to those with leadership roles in church (as pastor, Sunday School teacher, Bible study leader, musician …) it applies equally to anyone who calls themself a disciple of Christ.

Read verses 17–21 through again (ignoring any subheadings) and feel the shock of the request in verse 21.

Jesus has just told the disciples that he will be brutally killed, and yet they see this as the moment for self-advancement. What callous indifference to the sufferings of Christ! Maybe when Jesus predicted his death and resurrection, it was the resurrection that they focussed on, and they forgot the cross.

Jesus uses this incident to reveal their wrong understanding, and to show how discipleship and leadership are always cross-shaped. They want glory, but they haven't understood the suffering that must come first. This is how it was for Christ, and this is how it will be for us too.

Worldly leadership is characterised by 'lording it over' and 'exercising authority'. We know this too well as we see politicians and business leaders use their position to exploit others and gain personal advantage. 'Not so with you!' Jesus answers (v. 26). Christian ministry is to be utterly different.

Christ came to *serve*, not to be served. He gave his life for others, paying for their sins at the cross. As well as this being the basis of our salvation, it is the model for discipleship and Christian leadership. To seek status from our Christian ministry is to despise the cross of Christ, no matter how well we may proclaim it from the pulpit. To be a bully and lord it over those we lead is to deny the good news of Jesus, no matter how much we use the word 'gospel'. The true mark of understanding and treasuring the cross is that we serve others.

Pray this for your own church minsters. When choosing a church, find one where the minister not only preaches the cross, but lives by it. And to the extent that you have any leadership roles in church, resolve never to be self-serving, but lay down your privileges and rights for the sake of others. Such is the way of Christ.

REFLECTION

Pray now for your leaders.

Are there areas of life in which you need to repent?

If people never heard your words but only saw your example, what would they learn of Christ?

DAY 28

READ Matthew 21:1–22

Picture the scene: Jesus riding into Jerusalem on the donkey, with crowds laying palm branches before him. It is one of the most familiar images from the gospels, but that may mean we miss its shock and significance.

By riding the donkey, Jesus is clearly identifying himself with the king promised in Zechariah. But he is also showing what *sort* of king he is. There is no horse, no chariot, no show of power or strength. Jesus is a *humble* king.

The next section shows that Jesus' humility is not a 'weak' humility. In fact true humility is never weak. Rather, it is the using of strength for others, not for oneself. Jesus laid aside his glory, yet could not bear to see his Father dishonoured by the temple becoming a place of greed and corruption. There is real anger here. I remember a school-teacher of mine quoting this angry incident as a reason he couldn't accept Jesus; it shocked him. When we get close to the Jesus of the gospels, we may find we are shocked; we may find him challenging. He is bad news for religious leaders who put their own structures and selfishness in the way of true devotion. Yet he is gracious to the blind and lame, and indeed anyone else who comes to him acknowledging their need.

Take a moment to stand in awe of this king. Take a moment to repent of any ways you have turned faith in Christ to any end other than knowing God. Then marvel afresh that there is mercy to the blind, the lame, the needy like us.

In the final section of this passage, Jesus enacts a picture of what will happen to the temple. The temple is like the fig tree: it looks very leafy and flourishing, but there is no fruit. So, like the fig tree, it will be cursed and wither. It will no longer be the place where people meet with God and where sacrifices are made for sin. Praise Jesus for his judgment on false religion! Join the crowd in adoration of this humble yet mighty king!

REFLECTION

How does this passage enrich our view of Jesus?

Jesus died to end false religion, and to enable foreigners, the disabled and children to come to him. How are we reflecting his priorities?

DAY 29

READ Matthew 21:23–46

Jesus is the cornerstone, not an ornament. Like a building's cornerstone, he is big, awkward and hard to ignore; he is angular. He makes the whole building fit together, or else he is a colossal pain, constantly getting in the way. Is our Jesus like this? Or have we smoothed off the rough edges? If so, he won't offend, but nor will he be able to save.

The book of James reminds us that faith without deeds is dead. This parable of the two sons says something similar about our words: without deeds they too are dead. There is a general principle here that we should follow through on our words and keep our promises. In particular, though, Jesus is criticising the religious leaders of the day, who say the right things, but don't actually do the will of God. In fact it is the tax-collectors and prostitutes – who seem to be the most rebellious – who end up responding to Jesus and doing the will of God. This should challenge us today. Many may look the part and sound very religious, but salvation comes down to whether we have actually responded to God's call to repent and believe in Jesus.

The next parable focuses further on the Jewish leaders' rejection of Jesus. We see the entire history of Israel here. The vineyard represents the promised land given to Israel, itself an echo of the garden of Eden. Yet the tenants don't acknowledge that it is a gift they've received with obligations. Rather, they want it for their own. They want the gift but not the giver. They want creation but not the creator. The servants sent by the owner represent the prophets God sent his people to call them back to him. But they were beaten, killed and ignored.

Then the owner sends his son, and Jesus explains why he too will be killed: not because he isn't recognised; rather, *because* he is recognised as the son and heir, so the tenants kill him to get the vineyard for themselves. Jesus was rejected and killed because people realised he had a claim on their lives, and they hated that. The same is true today.

The Jesus of the gospels is awkward and uncomfortable. We either stumble over him, or find that he makes everything else fit together. Is the Jesus we believe in like this?

REFLECTION

Which aspects of Jesus' character and teaching are you tempted to 'smooth off' to make him more acceptable? What would be the result?

DAY 30

READ Matthew 22:1–14

What is the kingdom of heaven like? It is a feast, not a fast. It is a banquet all prepared. It is the fattened calf slaughtered and ready. In fact it is more than just any feast; it is a *wedding* feast – which in Jesus' day would have been even more extravagant than today – where no expense is spared. An occasion where everything is at its best. We enjoy this in part now, though we await Christ's return to know its full expression. Living God's way is never second best. Is this the kingdom of heaven we present to others? One that is a feast?

More than that, is the kingdom of heaven we present to others one that is centred on Jesus, as the wedding feast in the story is centred on the bridegroom? If what we are offering to people is a lifestyle choice, an optional extra to make their lives better, then it can't be very wrong to reject the gospel. However, if it is not first about me and my needs, but about Jesus, then things are different. The guests at this banquet will know great joy because first and foremost the banquet is about the bridegroom – Jesus.

This explains the king's anger. To refuse to come is to refuse to honour the son. The killing of the messengers is a picture of the people of Israel who killed the prophets and rejected God's call. The servants going to the streets picture God's kingdom being opened to all, irrespective of religious background. God's salvation of people from all nations is wonderful news for us, but it is first and foremost about his Son being honoured.

This also explains the expulsion of the guest not in wedding clothes. It is not just those who reject God outright who are left outside; it is also anyone who presumes to come, but isn't prepared to come on the king's terms. For us the king's terms are repentance and faith, a life of trust and obedience to Christ.

Have you come? Have you come on the king's terms? Or are there areas of life you refuse to submit to him. The kingdom of heaven is a feast, of great joy. But it is about Christ before it's about us. So come, not presumptuously but confidently. Come, not reluctantly but gladly.

REFLECTION

How does this passage change how we think about the future?

How could this passage shape our evangelism?

DAY 31

READ Matthew 22:15–46

Not all questions are good questions. How we need to understand this in a society where questioning is a virtue. Here two very different groups of people try to catch Jesus out with questions.

The first question is about *ethics*: how to live. The Pharisees try to put Jesus in a no-win situation. If Jesus says taxes to Caesar are lawful, this will lessen his popularity with his Jewish people. Yet if Jesus says paying taxes is not lawful, he will be in trouble with the Roman authorities.

Jesus takes the opportunity to point to the greater authority: God. Taxes may be due to Caesar; his image is on the coin. But all of humanity owes God a greater allegiance: our very selves. We are made bearing his image. This is where to start. Every ethical question ultimately depends on understanding and relating to God rightly. Only then can lesser questions be sorted out.

The Sadducees' question is about *doctrine*. They were the liberals of the day, who denied the resurrection. They invent this story about the seven brothers, trying to show that belief in the resurrection is ridiculous.

Jesus' response is striking. He criticises them for a conclusion (or inference) they fail to draw. God saying, 'I *am* the God of Abraham' (v. 32, my italics) should have led them to conclude there is a resurrection – Abraham is living, not dead. Though the Sadducees aren't contradicting Scripture directly, for Jesus denying a necessary implication from Scripture is to deny the Scriptures. Doctrine matters. Jesus requires us to read the different parts of Scripture together, each in light of the others.

Ultimately Jesus brings these questions back to the greatest question: 'What do you think about the Messiah?' (v. 42). Questions of ethics and doctrine have their place, but neither can be answered unless we first get Jesus' *identity* right. Every question of how to live and every difficult question of doctrine must be related to who Jesus is.

When we face tough questions like this from our society, can we do as Jesus did and move the discussion to his identity? As Christians we live the way we do because we love Jesus, and we believe what we do because Jesus makes sense of this world. 'What do you think about Christ?' is a good question to ask.

REFLECTION

Think of questions of ethics or doctrine that you struggle with. How does understanding who Jesus is help with these?

What do you think about the Messiah?

DAY 32

READ Matthew 23:1–24

Some today are nervous of church, nervous of religious authorities. Maybe they've been bruised, or even abused, by those in positions of spiritual authority. How encouraging this passage is for such people. No one receives stronger criticism from Jesus than those who misuse their power. As you re-read this passage, be warned by the negative example of the Pharisees. But also marvel at our Saviour and how he is the complete opposite to this.

The Pharisees may say what is true, but their lives don't match (vv. 2–3). This is the hypocrisy we all find so tempting. Yet Christ consistently lived out his own teaching: the beautiful embodiment of God's holy law to love God and love neighbour. The Pharisees lay burdens on others (v. 4). How sad when today we know people who dread going to church because of the burden that will be laid on them. Jesus, by contrast, carried our burdens; he bore our sins.

Pharisees do good only to be seen by others, to bring themselves glory (vv. 5–12). Jesus suffered outside the camp, in shame and disgrace, to bring *us* to glory. Pharisees love titles and status, but Jesus gave up his privileges, not counting equality with God something to be grasped. He became a servant, giving his life for us.

Pharisees gather followers to themselves, rather than point people to life in the kingdom of God (vv. 13–22). False religion leads people to death, but Jesus leads people to life. Pharisees are crafty with words, hedging their promises and sounding spiritual in the process. Jesus came speaking the truth, even when it was unpopular. If he kept his promise to die for his people, how much more will he keep every other promise he made!

Pharisees turn the law into a way of looking down on others, obsessing with the minutiae (vv. 23–24). Jesus says that the law was about care for people, and showed justice and mercy and faithfulness in abundance, such that he could be called 'friend of sinners'.

Oh that we would be kept free from the hypocrisy of the Pharisees and follow more closely in the footsteps of our Saviour! Imagine the impact of our evangelism if it was backed up with a church that was ruthless in rooting out its own hypocrisy, and radical in pursuing the justice, mercy and faithfulness that characterise our Lord. Praise him!

REFLECTION

What aspect of this passage challenges you most? What aspect of Jesus' character do you find most appealing?

DAY 33

READ Matthew 23:25–39

'Why are Christians such hypocrites?' We've probably all heard this question. The world around us hates seeing Christians who pretend to be moral, who speak out against the sin they see around them, but fail to address the sin in their own lives.

In this passage Jesus continues his harsh criticism of the Pharisees, and the issue is again their *hypocrisy*, the fact that their inside doesn't match their outside.

Pharisees clean the outside of the cup, that is they make themselves look very moral and respectable, but inside they are dirty (vv. 25–26). Worse than that, they are like whitewashed tombs (vv. 27–28). They are places of uncleanness, of death, yet they hide this and pretend to be pure. This is wicked enough in itself, but all the more so as it leads others astray. What a contrast to Christ, who was outwardly disfigured, who was numbered among sinners and thieves, who in fact became sin for us, while all the time being himself sinless.

The Pharisees' hypocrisy even extends to claiming to honour the very prophets whose message they so oppose (vv. 29–32). This is the heart of false religion: all the formality and structure, but none of the content. Note how *conservative* the Pharisees seem: building monuments, being in continuity with the past, saying the right things. But Jesus calls them a 'brood of vipers' (v. 33), dangerous, venomous.

They are showing themselves to be offspring of the serpent (Gen. 3:15), doing the will of the devil not the will of God. Because they hate God, they hate the good news about his Son, Jesus, and so they persecute and kill his messengers who speak of him. Jesus is rightly angry, but he is also compassionate. The false-teaching vipers load people down and lead them to hell. Jesus longs to gather this rebellious people under his wings like a mother hen (v. 37). It is not the image we would expect after the strong language of this passage.

Jesus confronts power and its abuse. He challenges hypocrisy. But he is compassionate and offers grace, even to hypocrites who have rebelled against him. Isn't this the sort of leader we long for? Isn't this the sort of leader to whom we can trust our very lives?

REFLECTION

Do we have Jesus' compassion over the lost? How could we increase this?

Are there areas in our lives where we are being hypocritical?

READ Matthew 24:1–28

How should we respond when the whole world seems to be falling apart? Natural disasters, terrorist incidents, senseless acts of violence, not to mention the threat of nuclear war that seems as severe as I write this as it has been for many years.

In this passage Jesus is speaking about the Roman army's attack on Jerusalem and the temple that would happen within the lifetime of his hearers. The lesson for them – and the lesson for us when facing similar earth-shattering events – is that the end is not yet. What seem to be signs of the end of the world are in fact only 'the beginning of birth-pains' (v. 8) – a sign that we are living in the last days.

This is an important message for them, and for us, because thinking the end is imminent may cause us to adopt a 'crisis' mentality that makes us more susceptible to false teaching: 'Watch out that no one deceives you' (v. 4).

So Jesus teaches that there will be great persecution and church decline, but warns his followers not to be unsettled by this (vv. 9–14). This isn't the sign of the end of the world. Quite the opposite: the gospel must go to *all nations* before the world ends! So they should stand firm, continuing to live the normal Christian life.

Likewise, Jesus speaks of the siege of Jerusalem (vv. 15–28). This took place in AD 66, prior to its total destruction in AD 70. The 'abomination that causes desolation' (v. 15) is hard to pinpoint exactly, but the equivalent passage in Luke links it to Jerusalem being surrounded by the Roman armies. If ever it would feel like the world was ending, this is it. But again the disciples are warned to stand firm, to beware false teaching. All the chaos might make false teachers look more persuasive. Maybe some would even cite the turmoil around them as part of their message. But this wasn't the end of the world. When Christ returns, it will be utterly unmistakable. Until then, stand firm.

Today we too need to beware false prophets who trade on the turmoil in the world to promote their message. When the world seems to be falling apart, we need to remember the end is not yet. We don't need a 'different gospel' for these unsettled times. We mustn't listen to 'doomsday prophets'. Keep living ordinary Christian lives of repentance and faith. Don't be led astray. Stand firm. And keep on with the task of taking the gospel to all nations.

REFLECTION

What place does the future have in your faith?

How does this passage say the future should affect life now?

DAY 35

READ Matthew 24:29–35

After the siege of Jerusalem, described in Matthew 24:4–28, verses 29–35 predict the destruction of the temple in AD 70, but do so in a symbolic not literal way. Rather than describing exactly how things will look, Jesus is giving the *theology* of these events, using language from the Old Testament.

The language is that of judgment. The image of the sun and moon being darkened comes from Isaiah 13:10, when judgment on Babylon is foretold. The image of stars falling comes from Isaiah 34:4, when judgment is pronounced on the nations. Here is not just the end of the temple, but also the end of earthly Jerusalem's place in God's plan. It now faces judgment like all the foreign nations.

The trumpet call references Isaiah 27:13, when a trumpet would announce the regathering of God's exiled people. Here it is not just the Jewish exiles but God's elect from all nations, 'from the four winds' (v. 31), who are being gathered. The destruction of Jerusalem is the final act in the changeover from Judaism to Christianity. The temple will no longer be where God's people meet with him. Salvation will no longer be limited to ethnic Israel, but the good news will go to all nations.

Verses 32 to 35 speak to the first disciples, saying that the tribulations described in the previous passage are a sign that the destruction of the temple and the missionary age of the church are near. How should we respond to these truths, living so long after AD 70?

First, if we're not Jewish, we should rejoice that salvation is no longer confined to ethnic Israel, and encountering God no longer limited to the temple. The destruction of the temple was the final end of Old Covenant religion. If we are Christians, we are those who have heard the trumpet call of the gospel, who are being gathered into God's kingdom.

Second, we should understand the days in which we live. The end is not yet. But the age of the church, the last days, has begun. Will you be part of the mission of the church? Will you be one of these messengers (that's what 'angel' in v. 31 means) involved in gathering God's elect from the four winds?

REFLECTION

Why hasn't Jesus returned yet?

How can you live in the light of the future?

DAY 36

READ Matthew 24:36 – 25:13

How do we get ready for Christ's return? So far Jesus has cautioned his hearers against a 'crisis' mentality that sees world upheaval as a sign of the imminent end. Such a way of living is dangerous as it makes us more easily led astray by false teaching. But how do we prepare for the end of the world? And when will it come?

'But about *that* day or hour no one knows' (24:36, my italics): Jesus now moves from speaking of the destruction of the temple to speaking of the end of the world. Final judgment will not be announced with signs, and cannot be predicted. In his humanity even Jesus Christ did not know the date of his return. How astonishing that Christians throughout history have presumed to determine the date.

Jesus is emphatic on this. Like in the days of Noah, when people were unaware of and not ready for the flood, so it will be with his return. The picture of two men in the field, with one taken, points again to the sudden division that will take place on that day, without warning.

Like the burglar, Jesus will not announce the hour of his arrival. It will be abrupt and unexpected! So Jesus tells his disciples to stay awake, to be ready. This is the point of the parable of the ten virgins. Five were ready (they had enough oil) and five were not. Once Jesus returns, it will be too late to repent. Salvation – like the oil – can't be passed from one person to another. Just because those around us are ready doesn't mean we are.

What does readiness look like? 24:13 spoke of standing firm to the end – keeping on living the ordinary Christian lives of repentance and faith. The wise servant (24:45) was ready for the return of his master because he was doing what his master had told him to do, rather than using his master's absence as an excuse to be self-serving and wicked.

Stay awake. Be ready, lest we be cast to pieces with the hypocrites, or be shut out of the banquet like the foolish virgins.

REFLECTION

Have you turned to Jesus in repentance and faith? If not, please don't delay. None of us knows how long we have.

If you're a Christian, are you living in the light of Christ's return? Are you busy doing his work, or are you using the delay to be self-seeking?

DAY 37

READ Matthew 25:14–30

The parable of the bags of gold (or 'talents', ESV) elaborates further what it means to be ready for Jesus' return: it means seeking wisely to steward the gifts he's given us. It also gives a striking lesson about our service of God: it flows from our view of God's character.

God is represented by the master in this story, and we learn several things about him. First, we see his generosity. A 'talent' was the highest unit of currency in Jesus' day. The servants are all given different amounts of money – representing the different gifts and opportunities God has given us to serve him with – but *all* are given an astonishingly large amount.

Second, we see that God rewards faithfulness. The first and second servants had earned different amounts, but the commendation they receive is the same. Those who serve God faithfully in this life will be given great opportunities for service in the next. This is part of what it means to 'Come and share your master's happiness!' (vv. 21, 23).

The final servant has not sought to invest the money. The reason given is that he thinks his master is harsh. He is motivated by fear. But how wrong his view of his master is!

If we think God to be generous and good, we will attempt *bold* things for him, knowing that he will generously reward faithful service, and also that there is grace for when we fail. We will be motivated by his smile, his commendation, his words 'Well done, good and faithful servant!'

But we must be warned if we have no desire at all to serve him. Beware that this does not reveal a heart that proves we don't know God. If so, we will be 'thrown outside, into the darkness, where there will be weeping and gnashing of teeth' (Matt. 8:12). A great separation is coming. It will be terrible on that day to be revealed as one who had no relationship with God.

Service of God is true freedom. Look at his character, revealed in Christ. Be ready for his return by serving him with all we are and all we have, knowing him to be generous.

REFLECTION

How does God's character motivate your service?

What are the gifts and circumstances God has given you that you could use to serve him?

DAY 38

READ Matthew 25:31–46

The scene painted here could hardly be more weighty or significant. We are given a glimpse of the final judgment when all will stand before Christ.

Jesus' teaching here directly challenges two views that are common in the church today. The first is that the Christian faith is simply about believing the right things, and not about what we *do*. Yet in this passage the word 'do' is repeated numerous times, and belief is not mentioned! If this feels wrong to us, it shows that our view of faith and discipleship may be out of step with that of Jesus. The faith that Jesus calls us to, the faith that saves us, is never 'mere belief'. It is faith that results in a changed life.

The second view that Jesus challenges is that only 'spiritual' things matter. Such a view owes more to pagan philosophy than the Bible. Throughout Matthew's gospel the all-encompassing nature of Christ's kingdom has been seen. We are to care for other Christians' *physical* as well as spiritual needs, as we follow the example of our master.

But as well as a challenge, there is a great encouragement here for Christians. Don't we wish we could have met Jesus face to face, and served him? Don't we wish we could have been there to express our love for him in practical ways? Wouldn't we have loved to have clothed him when he was naked, tended to him when he was sick, hosted him at our house like Zaccheaus did, shown him compassion when no one else seemed to? What an astounding privilege this would have been!

Yet this is what we can do as we minister to the needs of Christ's people. We are doing it for him. When we provide shelter for a displaced believer, open our home to the victim of domestic violence, give food to the hungry, break down racial and ethnic barriers even at great cost, reach out to provide safety for those exploited through the sex trade, all these things we do for *him*. We prepare for meeting Christ in his glory by meeting him in his humility and degradation. If we want to see the King of kings to whom all powers will bow, look among the lowest and the least.

REFLECTION

Is your faith a living faith that is expressed in deeds?

Who are the 'least of these' (v. 45) that you could serve? How?

DAY 39

READ Matthew 26:1–35

In the humble setting of a leper's home, a thing of great beauty happens. A woman takes a jar of expensive perfume and pours it on Jesus' feet. This is an extravagant act of devotion, as the perfume is worth about a year's wages. In this culture most people are poor, with little savings, so such an action is catastrophic financial planning. More than this, it seems to serve no *purpose*; think of all the good that could be done with the money.

Jesus radically reshapes our ideas of value. Far from being a waste, this outpouring is a 'beautiful thing' (v. 10). It is hard to think of anyone else in Scripture who receives as high praise as this. This woman never preaches a sermon, never plants a church, probably never darkens the corridors of power or influence. Humanly speaking, she achieves *nothing*. But she gives of herself to show her love for Jesus, and Jesus delights in that.

There is a wrong view of the Christian life that considers any good deeds we try to do for the Lord as 'filthy rags'. But that's not how Jesus sees this beautiful act of devotion, and he finds pleasure and beauty in our acts of devotion to him too.

What a contrast Judas is! He is in the inner circle. He eats with Jesus. Yet he gives Jesus up for thirty pieces of silver – just a few month's wages. The woman sees that Jesus is soon to die, and she responds with costly devotion. Judas sees that Jesus is soon to die, so tries to cut his losses by making a bit of money.

Do we see discipleship as about what we can *get* from Jesus? Or, like this woman, have we recognised who Jesus is (strikingly, Judas never calls Jesus 'Lord') and want to give ourselves in wholehearted devotion? Which of these two responses most characterises our discipleship?

The end of the passage (vv. 30–35) is both sobering and encouraging. Like the first disciples, we all fail Jesus in so many ways. But just as for them, for us there is grace beyond failure. We are not defined by our past. God's mercy is new every morning.

REFLECTION

What sort of disciple do you want to be today?

What could you do for Jesus that he might see as 'beautiful'?

Why do you think the woman responded this way to Jesus?

DAY 40

READ Matthew 26:36–56

'Go to dark Gethsemane'.[4] Linger there a while with Jesus. See his sorrow. Hear the agony as his voice catches as he speaks. Look on a frail man, a vulnerable man, a scared man. It's not a comfortable place to be, but it's a place we must be.

Nowhere in Scripture do we see the humanity of Jesus more clearly shown: 'My soul is overwhelmed with sorrow to the point of death' (v. 38). Jesus isn't exaggerating here. This is anguished honesty, a plea to his friends to be near him as he faces such unimaginable agony.

Hear his anguished prayer to the Father, asking if this cup may be taken from him. The 'cup' here symbolises divine judgment and points to the spiritual sufferings that will accompany and far outweigh the physical ones.

Throughout his life, Jesus has known suffering: hunger, thirst, rejection, grief and pain. But he has done so with the Father's smile upon him, with the verdict of 'well pleased' comforting him. Now he must do it alone. Now he must not simply live among sinners (itself an agony for one so pure) but be *made* sin, taking on himself the vileness and filth of human perversion. The smile of the Father will turn to the forsakenness of the Father, as he punishes Jesus with great and terrifying holiness.

This is what caused Jesus to shrink back with horror. This is what made him weak with dread. This is what made Jesus look for *any* other way: 'Yet not as I will, but as you will' (v. 39).

'Go to dark Gethsemane'. Linger there a while. Rightly we focus on the achievements of the cross: forgiveness, justification, eternal life. Let's celebrate those for eternity. But let's not forget the reality of the cross itself. Even that, though, is too abstract. Let's not forget *Jesus*. Look upon him. So weak. In such pain. So scared. So alone. And all for us. *This* is our God.

REFLECTION

Meditate for a while on what Christ endured for us.

Turn those thoughts into praise.

DAY 41

READ Matthew 26:57 – 27:10

The trial of Jesus is less about Jesus being on trial than about all of humanity being on trial. It reveals our hopelessness and guilt.

Jesus' trial before the Jewish authorities is illegitimate in so many ways. Trials were not supposed to happen at night, nor during the feast, nor were they supposed to take place in the house of the high priest. No guilty verdict should have been given without the chance for witnesses to speak on behalf of the accused. The council make an appearance of wanting to weigh the evidence, to do justice, but in fact they have decided the verdict before they even meet: 'The chief priests and the whole Sanhedrin were looking for false evidence against Jesus so that they could put him to death' (v. 59).

Scripture testifies that people are no different today. There are no 'neutral' observers of Jesus. There is no objective weighing of evidence. We all naturally reject Jesus because we don't like his claims on our lives. It's then just a question of finding enough 'evidence' to justify this verdict. We must be aware of this tendency in our own lives, and also in the lives of those we want to tell about Jesus. What wretches we are! How we need a Saviour who can transform rebellious hearts! Come to him.

Peter is a follower of Jesus, but self-preservation leads him to deny Jesus. He is willing to follow, but when it gets hard, when it really costs him, he turns back. If even one of Jesus' closest followers can fail him like this, so can we. How we need a Saviour who gives second and third and three hundredth chances to weak disciples like Peter and like us! Come to him.

Judas is tragic. He demonstrates regret, but not repentance. He realises he has done wrong, but he doesn't come to the one who can forgive even the greatest transgression. His remorse leads to despair and death, not to repentance and forgiveness. How we need a Saviour who pays for even the worst sins! Even Judas could have been forgiven. And so can we, no matter what we've done, how horrendous it is. When confronted with our sin, don't run and hide! Come to him. The cross reveals our sin, but also our only and glorious hope!

REFLECTION

What sins do we need to confess right now?

Spend some time meditating on Christ's mercy even to failed disciples.

DAY 42

READ Matthew 27:11–26

Put yourself in the place of Barabbas. From the other gospels we know he had been arrested for robbery, insurrection and murder. He had been sentenced to death. Perhaps he had a family who he thought he had seen for the last time. His life was over, without hope. What would he be thinking as he languished in prison waiting for his execution?

By the end of the passage, he has been released, and Jesus has been delivered to be crucified. A guilty man walks free, and an innocent man goes to his death. Matthew is surely wanting us to see the connection.

We don't know how much Barabbas knew of the deliberations that led to him being freed. We don't know if he knew anything of Jesus the innocent. We don't know if he knew that his freedom was dependent on Jesus' death. But if he had seen the full picture, he would have been able to say to his family, 'I'm alive today because another went to be crucified instead. An innocent man died today, and I have been set free.'

We will never understand the gospel of Jesus Christ unless we see ourselves in Barabbas' shoes. Unless we see that we, though perhaps not as openly rebellious as Barabbas, are nonetheless those who deserve God's judgment. Unless we see that justice would have us suffer the just punishment for our rebellion against God. Without Christ we would be as hopeless as Barabbas. But just as Christ died in the place of Barabbas, so Christ has died in our place if we trust in him. We have life because another died in our place. He was condemned so we could be set free.

Insert your own name in verse 26, seeing what the Father has done for you: 'Then he released ______________ to them. But he had Jesus flogged, and handed him over to be crucified.'

REFLECTION

Have you been a Christian so long that you have become overfamiliar with the wonder of Christ dying in your place? Pray that he might help you delight in this afresh.

READ Matthew 27:27–31

The cross isn't just something God *did*; it is an expression of who he *is*. The cross isn't a departure from his normal character. Rather, at the cross we see *most clearly* what God is like.

Picture the scene described in verses 27–31. Jesus has already been flogged (27:26): beaten with a whip to which pieces of metal and bone are attached, which has torn through his flesh, even exposing his internal organs. By the time he reaches the governor's headquarters, Jesus is incredibly weak, his life already draining away.

The Romans clothe this pitiful figure in red robes as an ironic sign of royalty. They place a crown on his head, but make it a crown of thorns to further increase the agony. They bow down and pay mock homage to him. Their message is clear: he claims to be a king, but he could not be any less like a king. They think his weakness, his pain and his blood all make his claims to kingship ridiculous. 'Nothing could be *less* kingly than this,' say the Romans. 'He's a disgrace.' Nothing could be *more* kingly, says the Father: 'I am well pleased with him.'

Jesus' glory is most clearly seen in the humiliation of the cross. His kingship is most clearly seen in his death. The Romans mean to mock him, but in fact they point to the very heart of who he is and what sort of king he is. If you want to know what God is like, look at this frail man pouring out his life for others. If you want to understand kingship, gaze on the crown of thorns.

The story of the cross is one that we'd never dream of or imagine. It's astounding that one so high should become so low. It's almost unthinkable that the Creator of all things, who holds worlds in his hands, should enter our world and do so in order to die. But, at another level, it's not surprising at all. This is what God has *always* been like. *So* good. *So* loving. *So* generous. Dying for his people is utterly consistent with his character. It's *exactly* the sort of thing he'd do.

REFLECTION

Spend some time meditating on the love and generosity of Christ.

Now imagine what it will be like to have him spend an eternity loving us and doing us good (Eph. 2:7).

DAY 44

READ Matthew 27:32–44

The cross is bad news for us before it is good news. It humbles us before it assures us. We see both these emphases in this passage.

The cross shows us the depths of our sin. Matthew records a vast range of people who insult and mock Jesus: the passers-by, the religious leaders, even the criminals crucified with him. Add to this the Roman soldiers from the previous passage, the crowds who cried 'crucify him!' and even Peter who denied Jesus, and we have a picture of a man who has been rejected by the whole world. Much as we like to think we'd have been different, in fact we'd have been there among the mockers, we'd have been crying, 'Crucify him!' Mel Gibson vividly made this point in his film *The Passion of the Christ*; although he did not star in the movie, his one cameo was his hands hammering the nails through Jesus' hands and feet. 'I did this,' he was saying, and we all must say the same.

Jesus died because of my sin. What a terrifying and humbling thought that I should be so wicked. It should drive me to my knees.

But the cross also assures us. Think of the 'written charge' nailed to Christ's cross (v. 37). This was the crime for which the person was being punished: in Jesus' case his claim to be king of the Jews. Paul picks up this image in Colossians 2:14, saying that *our* charge sheet – the list of all the sins for which we should be condemned – has been nailed to Christ's cross. When your sin haunts you, when you hear Satan's accusations, look up to the cross. See on that charge sheet *your* sins, all the things you're most ashamed of. See beneath that list of sins a bloody Saviour saying, 'I have died for these sins. Justice has been satisfied. Those sins have been paid for. There is *no* condemnation left for my people.'

Jesus died for my sin. What a glorious thought that I should be so loved. It should lift me to my feet in praise.

REFLECTION

Spend some time now confessing your sins for which Christ died.

Then mentally place that list of sins above Jesus' head on the cross, as sins for which he has paid in full.

DAY 45

READ Matthew 27:45–66

Matthew doesn't focus on the physical agony of the cross. Rather, he focuses on four events that bring out its spiritual significance.

First, **the darkness**. God had promised through Amos that when he came to judge, he would 'make the sun go down at noon and darken the earth in broad daylight' (Amos 8:9). Though Jesus was sinless, as he died he was paying the penalty for the sins of his people; he was enduring the fearsome judgment we all deserve.

Second, **Jesus' cry** further explains what this judgment was like: it was nothing less than being forsaken by God. We mustn't try to explain away this verse, or dull its force. Yes, Jesus died according to God's plan. Yes, the Trinitarian bonds between Father and Son remained intact. Yes, Jesus knew that after his death lay resurrection. But none of these facts diminish the reality that Jesus really was forsaken by God. He really did suffer the agony of relational separation from his Father. Instead of God's smiling face, he really did experience his fierce disapproval and condemnation. This is the mystery and glory of the incarnation! How is it possible for God to suffer? How is it possible for the Son to be forsaken by the Father? Jesus became man to make these things possible. He took on flesh so that he could have such experiences that would be unthinkable for God.

As Jesus dies, the next events show third what his death achieved. **The temple curtain** guarded the way to the Holy of Holies, the place of God's presence. The curtain was decorated with gigantic cherubim, echoing the cherubim that guarded the way back into the Garden of Eden after Adam and Eve had been cast out. As the temple curtain was torn in two, this showed that the way was open for humanity to be in God's presence, to return to Eden.

Fourth, the earthquake and the **raising of the dead bodies** point to the life we receive through Jesus' death. Language of earthquakes and splitting rocks is – like language of darkness – used in the prophets to describe the day of judgment. But now Jesus has faced the punishment for the sins of his people, this future day of judgment will not be one of condemnation, but of *life*.

He was forsaken, so we might be brought near. He faced judgment, so we might have life.

REFLECTION

Spend some time praising God for what the cross cost him, and what it achieved.

DAY 46

READ Matthew 28:1–20

It's very tempting to break Matthew 28 into two sections, dealing with the resurrection first, then the great commission. But Matthew intends us to see how the great commission flows out of the fact that Jesus is risen.

Jesus' commission to his disciples begins by him explaining, 'All authority on heaven and on earth has been given to me' (v. 18). Throughout Matthew's gospel Jesus' amazing authority has been seen, but at his resurrection the Father installs Jesus in a place of *all* authority, as the risen king. It is this authority that means he can command his disciples to 'go and make disciples of all nations' (v. 19). Jesus is the one before whom every knee will one day bow, and he calls his disciples to spread the gospel so that people come to Christ willingly now, rather than on the day of judgment as rebels waiting condemnation.

Are you a disciple of Jesus? Are you one of his followers? If not, what is stopping you coming to him? Look back through Matthew's gospel and see his authority. Do you see his claim on your life? Look back and see his goodness and compassion. Is this someone you would want to rule over you? Look back at the gloriously high standard of his ethical teaching. Would you dare stand on the day of judgment trusting in your own merits, rather than trusting in his sacrifice in your place?

If you are a disciple, note what discipleship is supposed to involve. First, being baptised, the sign of death and new life in Christ. Second, growing in obedience to everything Christ has commanded. Have you been baptised? Are you seeking daily to grow in the obedience that flows from your faith?

Third, by implication, being a disciple involves passing the message on, helping others come to faith and then grow in obedience. This should flow naturally from our understanding of who Jesus is, like Peter and John saying, 'we cannot help speaking about what we have seen and heard' (Acts 4:20).

The gospel ends, as it began, with a glorious promise of God's presence: 'surely I am with you always, to the very end of the age' (v. 20; cf. 1:23). Consider beginning every day remembering these truths: Christ is risen! Christ is with me! Let these fuel your joyful obedience, and mission to the world.

REFLECTION

Meditate on what Christ's resurrection means for his identity.

Meditate on what it means for our life of discipleship and mission.

REFERENCES

1 Thanks to Andy Robinson for this insight, which he learned from Hugh Palmer.

2 Andy Robinson suggested these very helpful questions to me.

3 Jason Mandryk, *Operation World* (IVP, 2012); Daphne Spraggett with Jill Johnstone, *Window on the World* (IVP, 2006).

4 'Go to dark Gethsemane' is a hymn by James Montgomery (1825).

MORE IN THIS SERIES

ROMANS
Momentous News
By David Cook
ISBN: 978-1-906173-24-1

MARK
The Suffering Servant
By Jeremy McQuoid
ISBN: 978-1-906173-55-5

DANIEL
Far From Home
By Justin Mote
ISBN: 978-1-906173-68-5

1 THESSALONIANS
Living for Jesus
By Julia Marsden
ISBN: 978-1-906173-67-8

PHILIPPIANS
Press Towards the Goal
By Kay Mumford
ISBN: 978-1-909611-31-3

GALATIANS
The Life I Now Live
By Peter Mead
ISBN: 978-1-910587-09-6

ACTS
To the Ends of the Earth
By David Cook
ISBN: 978-1-909611-02-3

EZEKIEL
For His Glory
By Peter Lau
ISBN: 978-1-909611-83-2

JOHN
Never Thirst Again
By David Cook
ISBN: 978-1-909611-30-6

and more at... 10 Publishing
a division of 10 of those.com

To place an order call: **0330 2233 423** email: **sales@10ofthose.com**
or order online: **www.10ofthose.com**